menorca

KU-444-632

Text by:
Francisco Tayá Pugés

© **Distribuciones SEBAS**
Balmes, 32 - Tel. 971 - 37 28 57
07730 ALAIOR (Menorca)

Impresión: Imdeart, S.A.
Salzillo, nave 6
Sant Adrià de Besós (Barcelona)
PHOTOGRAPH:
Carlos Rivas: Cover, countercover and page, 1, 7, 8, 10, 11 ▲, 13, 14, 19 ▲, 21, 22, 23, 24, 25, 26-27, 28, 29, 30, 31, 32, 33 ▲, 34, 35, 36, 37, 38, 39, 40-41, 42, 43, 44, 45, 46, 47, 48-49, 50, 51, 52, 53, 54, 55, 56-57, 58, 59, 60, 61, 62, 63, 64, 65, 66, 67, 68, 69, 70, 71, 72, 73, 74, 75 ▼, 79, 80, 81, 82, 83, 84, 85, 88, 89, 90, 92, 95, 99.
Foto Video J. Carreras: page; 9, 15, 18, 20, 93, 94.
Manuel Taltavull : page; 19 ▼, 87.

I.S.B.N.: 84-604-5368-5
Dep. Legal B. 8.438-XXXVI

MENORCAN ROMANCE

by Gumersindo Riera

She was an enchanted island, lost in the midst of the sea ...

The north wind, riding horseback on the crystal-clear waves, lashed her with stormy fury, carrying off in its great wings white sea-foam, full of salt and iodine ... and of dreams of the moon.

Sometimes the wind would cease, tired of lashing her coastal cliffs, which would never yield, neither to the rage of the sea, nor to the fury of the winds ... Ah, she was strong, very strong, that island earth.

So when the voice of the wind and the sea, with its echoes of eternity, grew silent, the isle would become a peaceful haven, with sweet murmurs of madrigals to ring the hours of day.

She was an enchanted island, lost in the midst of the sea ...

Her people -stern and bronzed- lived their lives wedded to their tasks, knowing nothing of other lands, of other skies or other seas, because for them there was no other world beyond their own.

Their ancient monuments -the stones paled by antiquity- reached towards the sky in secular silence, spreading throughout the islan the feeling of nostalgia for all things passings which can never return.

Was that island but a dream, in sleep which would never be awakened? It was a memory, a rhyme, nothing more than a magic spell; she was the legendary soul of the winds and of the sea; she was History, which lives eternally and will never die.

Across all the ever-succeeding centuries that isolated island remains firmer than ever. Should you one day visit her, remember when you do that she was once an enchanted island, lost in the midst of the sea...

(Prose translation of the prelude to the lyrical story in verse,
by Gumersindo Riera, "She was an Enchanted Island")

Ediciones Savir, S.A.
Barcelona

INTRODUCTION

Means of transport are becoming more rapid and more comfortable almost every day. Innumerable travel agencies will arrange a pleasant holiday in Menorca for you without the slightest effort on your part. And like every visitor to the island you will henceforward join the band of enthusiastic propagandists of what has become known as "the white and blue island", or (because it is shaped like a ship, eternally ploughing its way through the waves towards the east), "the ship island". But the most apt description of Menorca would be simply "the island of peace".

It is a fact that Menorca is still the least known and least frequented of the Balearics. What are the reasons for this? Possibly the half-truths enshrined in such phrases as "the island of stones and wind", or "the rock strewn with earth" have had their influence. Among the Spanish themselves, the name Menorca may evoke not very pleasant memories of military service in the fortress of La Mola. Moreover, there are, unfortunately, many people who get the islands mixed up and many is the Menorquin who has had to correct the remark, "Oh, so you're a Menorquin. You must be from Mallorca, then. It's all the same, isn't it?"

No, it certainly is not all the same. The Balearic islands are not similar to each other. Menorca, in particular, has many unique characteristics. It differs both from Mallorca and from Ibiza, because of its position, its geology, its landscape, its towns, its history and above all the character of its people.

The basic facts about Menorca, which any text-book of geography will tell you, are cold and bare: 47'8 km. long by 19'5 broad at the widest point; area (incluiding the small adjacent islets) 701'840 sq. km.; slight vegetation, absence of flowing rivers, slightly undulating hinterland with maximum height (at El Toro) of only 357'96 m.; population, in round figures, 62.000 distributed in two major towns (Maó and Ciutadella), six smaller towns with their own municipalities (Alaior, Ferrerías, Es Mercadal, Sant Lluís, Es Castell and Es Migjorn Gran), two villages (Fornells and Sant Climent) and several agricultural populated places such as Llucmassanas, San Juan de Carbonell, Torret and S'Uestra.

But do we really get to know Menorca from these basic facts? Of course not. The best way to begin a real study of Menorca is from the air. As you fly over the island you look down as though at a marvellous relief map; in this way you really begin to appreciate its hills and its planes, its woods of pine and oak and its streches of cultivated farmland with the curious patterns made by the dry-stone walls dividing the fields; its beautiful villages and its white farm-houses, most of them with graceful, whitewashed arches over the front door and some of them given additional character by an ancient tower built as a defence against Muslim pirate raids. All this you will observe in the most splendid sunlight, through a clear, unpolluted atmosphere, unequalled in the intensity of its blueness anywhere else. Indeed, Menorca's air, with its content of salt and iodine, its radiant luminosity, affects people -especially those accustomed to grey, misty climates- in a manner more stimulating and intoxicating than sparkling wine!

Once you have got a bird's-eye view of the island in this way you will begin the pleasurable and entirely personal task of discovering your Menorca and so proving yet again the superiority of the taste of fruit picked with your own hands over that served by a waiter in a hotel. And to savour the quiet, shy beauty of Menorca you will have very often to leave the main roads and go off through the pine-woods, down sandy footpaths which will lead you to some deep ravine with prehistoric caves in the high cliffs on either side, or to a peaceful beach which will fill you with enchantment. In the island's long, indented coast-line you will find innumerable coves, bays and natural harbours of every shape and size and to every taste. There are long, narrow coves remiscent of Scandinavian fiords; others, surrounded by dark boulders, between which bushes, often distorted by the winds, grasp for a foothold, seem to be the very image of Britanny.

But most of them are semi-circles of very fine, white sand, on which the waves break in gentle, irridescent crystals, turning one's thoughts to old tales of sunken anforae. Many of them have sonorous Arabic names such as Galdana, Binidali, Algaiarens, Canassía.* Some are still virgin beaches, as if they had just been formed; but the vast majority have now been "urbanized", which means that you may enjoy both the beauty and peace of the countryside and at the same time the most sophisticated requirements of contemporary living. And in all these bays the clear water takes on different hues according to the time of day, the season of the year and the vegetative and geological environment. And everywhere you go you will find a certain serenity, a sense of well-being -that "sosophrine" which the Greeks regarded as one of the great happinesses of man- which, more than the sun and sea air alone, will bring tranquility to mind and body in a most beneficient and relaxing manner.

*Galdana from the Arabic. Wadi, a river valley; Bini, the sons of.

For the cultivated visitor there are other aspects of Menorca -socio-economic, archeological, historical and so on- which he finds of greater interest than sun and countryside alone. This little book will endeavour to meet the needs of this type of reader by references to such matters as the special characteristics of the peoples of each town on the island, the marvellous abundance of its megalithic monuments and the various traces left in the life of the island by its different foreign conquerors. For example, the displays of horsemanship, which are the central feature of so many Menorcan feast-days and which are, perhaps, relics of the Arabic predilection for horses. Place names, too, so often go back to Arabic origins; for example, to add to those already mentioned, Binimaimut, Binigafull, Alfuri. The "good Catalán folk", whom Alphonso III called upon to re-populate the island after his conquest of the Moors in 1287 provided the principal racial and linguistic bases of Menorca, which even to-day feels much closer ties, both cultural and economic, with Barcelona than with Palma, its administrative capital. And the three British occupations of the XVIII century left very definite influences -especially in Maó- on the character of the people, in their language and on their architecture.

The character of the people of any country can be fully understood only by a study of their history. For this reason the final section of this little book is devoted to a survey -brief, but comprehensive in its general outline- of Menorca's complex past. Thus what began with the physical delight of enjoying Menorcan sun and sea will end with the more recondite pleasure of entering into the soul of a people: in this way you will come to love what began by giving you simple pleasure.

Puerto de Maó

MAÓ

"All roads lead to Rome", as the old saying goes. Menorca, too, may be reached in a number of ways.

The most popular, nowadays, is, of course, to come by air. The number of charter flights to Menorca from almost every country in Europe seems to increase almost daily. You get into your jet plane at Heathrow, Gatwick, or other airport, and you have hardly had time to eat the meal provided and read an article in your paper before you hear the conventional words over the loudspeakers: "Ladies and gentlemen, fasten your seat-belts, we are just about to land in the airport of Menorca. We hope you have enjoyed your flight, etc., etc...". But before you land don't forget the advice we gave you in the Introduction: try to get, through the cabin windows, a rapid glimpse of Menorca as a whole, then, during your stay, set about "conquering" it bit by bit and you will find il will lead you from one pleasant surprise to another.

If you have the use of a yacht while you are here you can drop anchor in the bay you like best, be it urbanized or untouched by man. Or you may wish to moor in the marvellous natural harbour of Fornells, or the narrower but equally delightful one of Addaia.

For many, however, the traditional sea route to Menorca is the best one of all and if you come from Barcelona you will cross in one of the comfortable car ferries which leave there on alternate evenings during the week (more often during the high season) and reach Maó in the early hours of the following morning. No other means of transport can offer anything to match that dawn entry into the magnificent port of Maó: it is an experience you will never forget.

We deliberately referred to to the "traditional" sea route, because the port of Maó has a remarkable evocative power. It was throughout the centuries the gateway to Menorca and the scene of much of the island's history. From the time when Phoenecian vessels called here with their cargos of purple cloth from Sidon, until the foreign dominations of the XVIII century, the name Port Maó meant Menorca.

Maó detail harbour

Maó harbour. Island del Roy

A number of historians regard the name Maó as derived from that of the Carthaginian general, Magón. Learned scholars of Semitic languages incline rather to the etymology of the word "Maguén", signifying "shield" or "protection", because of the security which its port -the finest and safest of all in the Mediterranean- provided to the ships of the Carthaginian navy.

But let us turn to watch the day break from our vantage point on the deck of our ship. At first there is hardly light enough for us to distinguish more than the bare outline of the rather narrow entry to the bay. Then, as the light increases in intensity, we can make out the severe walls of the ancient Lazareto, theatre in olden times of so many tragedies, but to-day a smiling holiday resort for the personnel of the Spanish health service. Behind it may be seen the outline of the fortres of Isabel II, known as La Mola and on the opposite side of the bay the ruins of the fortress of San Felipe and then the fishing village of Es Castell, which enjoys, among other things, the honour of being the most easterly village in the whole of Spanish territory.

The beautiful colours of the sunrise reflected in the water will fill you with admiration. You will observe now that the smooth water of the port begins to widen. On its shores can be seen elegant white chalets and hotels.

Bridge of San Roque

Detail Maó harbour

As you pass Es Castell on your left you will see on your right the Isla del Rey, the King's Island, so called because it was here that Alphonso landed in 1287 at the head of his army of conquest to expel the Moors. Later, in the XVIII century, it became known as "Bloody Island" because on it the English established a military hospital, which remained there when the island was returned to Spain and in fact was still used by the Spanish military autorities until 1964, when the present hospital on the main road to the airport was built. Lastyl, on the left, towards the uppermost reaches of the bay, you will perceive Maó itself, looking particularly fine in the rays of the early morning sun, sitting loftily on the slopes of its fortified hill, crowned with the towers and domes of its churches and its new multistorey blocks.

When you get ashore you will find it worth while taking a further, more leisurely look at the port. Three vantage points may be specially recommended for this purpose: Plaza Miranda, the wall near the entrance to the church of San Francisco, or the balcony reached by small street adjacent to the Ayuntamiento (Town Hall) which retains the poetic name of Calle del Puente del Castillo (the street of the bridge of the castle), so evocative of mediaeval associations. But if you want to capture the whole grandeur of the port of Maó there is an even more strategic point for this purpose than those we have already mentioned: from the lordly farmhouse of San Antonio, built on a hill on the other side of the port itself. The building is in neo-classic style and because of its spendid position became known during the period of English

Maó : Door to the sea

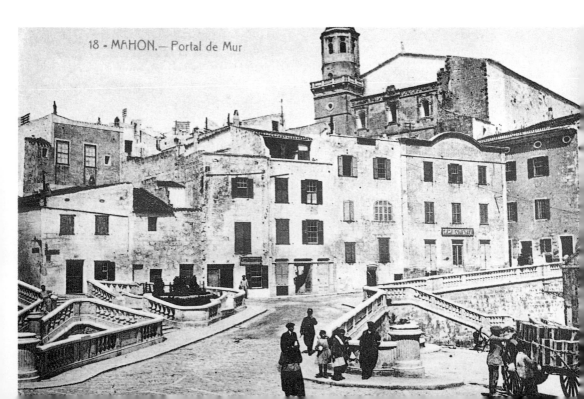

18 - MAHON.— Portal de Mur

rule as The Golden Farm. Later it became associated with the Nelson legent and indeed is often referred to as Nelson's house, because the great admiral is said to have spent four days there when he visited Menorca in 1797. Legend has it that Lady Hamilton was with him at the time, but is cannot, it would appear, be historically proved: evidently Menorcan legend-builders wanted a counterpart to the stay of the no less famous couple in Valldemosa, Mallorca: Chopin and Georges Sand. At all events, the Golden Farm has witnessed many great happenings in Menorca's history and these are immortalised in the famous "Stories of the Golden Farm", the author of which is the present owner of the farm.

Maó is built, as we have already mentioned, on the slopes of a rocky hill so you will not be surprised to find that many of its streets are steep: Deyá, for example. Another is one of the most popular and crowded shopping centres, Calle Hannover, named after the German dynasty of that name, members of which occupied the English throne during the period when Menorca belonged to Great Britain.

England left an indelible impression on Maó since, in 1722, the Governor, Sir Richard Kane, made it the capital instead of Ciutadella, which had had that honour since the time of the Moorish domination. British officials did much for Maó and its inhabitants thrived as a result of the brisk business they were enabled to do under the protection of the British fleet and with the further stimulus of the money brought in by the sailors and soldiers of His Gracious Britannic Majesty -and by corsaires and pirates. Thus began a rich and influential bourgeois class, liberal in its views as a result of contacts with many people from the outside world who passed through Maó during their travels on ships of all flags, or with refugees from the French revolution or the Napoleonic wars who took up residence in the Menorcan capital. Later on the town lost its cosmopolitan character and public officials and military men were to be seen walking through its hilly streets. At the beginning of the XIX century there was virtually no industry in Maó, but now it boasts of an "industrial polygon", where light industry is concertrated.

Old Maó has some notable public monuments. There are mediaeval remains, such as the Portal de San Roque , one of the ancient gateways in the city walls, defended by a castellated bastion; or the ancient lane which leads down to the port from Calle Isabel II near the military Governor's palace. (Some writers maintain that the arches in this lane are of Arabic origin, others consider them to date from the XVI century). One church worthy of note is ojival in outer appearace but its plan is that of a Greek cross; it was in fact built in the middle of the XVIII century as a Greek Orthodox church, dedicated to Saint Nicolas de Mira, by the Greek community, made up of ships; suppliers and business-men who flourished in Maó at that time, taking advantage of the freedom of worship under the British Crown to build a temple to their own faith. Now it is the sub-parish church of La Concepción. It is the only church in Spain to have started life as a Greek, temple and this, as we have seen is due to the peculiarities of Menorca's history. Outside the centre of the town the hermitage of the Virgen de Gracia (patron saint of Maó) presents a contrast in architectural styles between its XV century nave -with some delightful statues of Mary and of the archangel Gabriel- and the opulent baroque of its main chapel and the treasury.

Worthy of special mention is the monumental organ in the parish church of Santa María . This organ was built in Barcelona by the Swiss organ-builder, Kyburz, during the time of the Peninsular war and transported to Maó in 1809 with the special protection of the Commander-in-Chief of the British Mediterranean fleet, Admiral the Earl of Collingwood. It is one of the finest of its type in the world, has undergone a number of restorations (the latest in 1973) and the British magazine, Musical Times, devoted an article to its history in their March 1973 issue. Most travel agencies include a visit to the Santa María church in their programme of tours.

Maó, more than anywhere else in Menorca, has, of course, felt the stimulus of intellectual curiosity consequent upon the foreign dominations of the XVIII century During the second British domination (1768-82) an academy

Cales Fonts

charged with the care of Catalán grammar and literature was founded in Maó; this was at a time when the quality of the Catalán language as spoken on the mainland had decayed considerably and gives substance to the Menorcan boast that their own language is purer than Catalán itself. Many sons of Maó have become famous and brought honour to the hometown: Dr. Mateo Orfila, 1787-1853 (whose bust you will have observed in the steet which bears his name) was a well-known toxicologist ("the father of modern legal medicine") who became Professor of Chemistry in the medical faculty of the University of Paris; painters such as Pascual Calbo, naturalists like Francisco Cardona, composers such as Alaquer and Andreu and historians like Riudavets, Ramis y Ramis, Camps and Hernández-Sanz. At the present time the intellectual aspirations of Maó are enshrined in two institutions: one, the Scientific, Literary and Artistic Ateneo, usually known simply as the Ateneo, it contains a natural history museum, a library and a small auditorium where periodic concerts are held, often with artists of international repute; the other is the Casa de Cultura , where there is a well-laid-out museum, a library (in the ante-room to which is a collection of old books and documents relating mainly to the British occupations, known as the Jim Maps collection), the town archives (where many a historian, past and present, has spent hours of patient research) and, in the basement, a small concert auditorium with excellent acoustics.

Detail Maó harbour

14

▲ Rivermouth Maó harbour. Island Lazareto ▼

ACROSS THE ISLAND

Look again, for a moment, at the map of Menorca and notice the location of its various towns.In the south-east region there are three: Es Castell, Sant Lluís and Sant Climent. Then, following the main road westwards towards Ciutadella, you come first to Alaior, then, in the geographical centre of the island, Es Mercadal. The termino (or rural district) of Es Mercadal with one further village within its boundaries: Fornells, in the north Es Migjorn Gran lies in the south.

Then, again following the main road, you reach Ferreries and finally, after a further 16 km., Ciutadella.

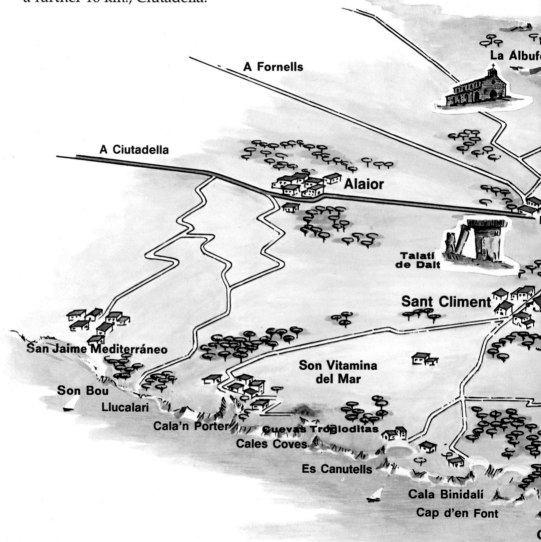

A Fornells

La Álbufe

A Ciutadella

Alaior

Talatí
de Dalt

Sant Climent

San Jaime Mediterráneo

Son Vitamina
del Mar

Son Bou

Llucalari

Cala'n Porter

Cuevas Trogloditas

Cales Coves

Es Canutells

Cala Binidalí

Cap d'en Font

C

All these towns differ from each other in their historical origins, in the character of their people and even in the particular version of the Menorquin language spoken by them. All are worthy of a visit to get to know the points of historic and touristic interest both in the towns themselves and their "términos". Let us begin with the three nearest Maó.

Es Castell originated with the collection of houses built for the families of military personnel just outside the main fortified walls of the great fortress of Saint Felipe* and known as La Arrabal (the suburb), or St. Philip's Town; howerer, it was found to interfere with military operations and was transferred to its present site by the British, who renamed it George Town, after King George III: this is the reason why you will see in the armorial bearings of the town the image of Saint George, patron saint of England. During the brief

* For the history of this fortress see final section.

Isla Colom

Es Grao

Sa Mesquida

Cabo Negro

Cala Llonga

Isla del Rey

Lazareto   La Mola

Punta del
Esperó

MAÓ   Es Castell

Talayot
de Trepucó

Cala de San Esteban

Aeropuerto

Sant Lluis   Rafalet

Torret

S'Uestrá   S'Algar

Cala Alcaufar

Las Lomas   Punta Prima

Binibeca   Biniancolla

safulla

Isla del Aire

17

General view: La Mola, Lazareto, Maó

period of Spanish occupation of the XVIII century (1782-1798) it became known as La Villa Real de San Carlos, after Charles III of Spain and Es Castell it has remained ever since. It looks directly across the port of Maó, commanding an excellent view of the three islands -Lazareto, Cuarentina and Isla del Rey- and of the Golden Farm, high over the opposite shore. It has two small natural harbours of its own, Cala Fonts and Cala Corp.

The town is modern in its layout and is built round a large central square, or "Champ de Mars", and surrounded by military barracks and offices in typical British Colonial style of the XVIII century, now bearing names such as Duque de Crillón and Cifuentes. Here it was that the ceremony took place, in 1802, of the handing over of Menorca to the Spanish, immortalised in a painting by Chiesa. One of the buildings, with a clock tower, is now the Ayuntamiento. In the past Es Castell, as well as being a military centre, was a town of fishermen and brave sea-farers, the modern descendants of whom, while still following the trades of their forebears to some extent, now tend to seek their livelihoods and their diversions in neighbouring Maó. The people of Es Castell have more names of mainland (or "peninsula") origin than those of any other town in Menorca, a legacy of the soldiers who, from the XVI to the XVIII centuries, founded their families while garisoned in the nearby fortress of San Felipe. One of the greatest of Menorcan writers, both in poetry and prose, in Castillan, Catalán and Menorquin, Angel Ruiz, was a native of Es Castell.

Part of the harbour ▲

Inside Lazareto ▼

A short distance from Es Castell the ruined walls and underground galleries and, incidentally, the original tomb of Sir Richard Kane, may still be seen in the remains of the Fortress of San Felipe*. They will give you some idea of its immensity and of its significance in the history of Menorca throughout three centuries.

Sant Lluís -perhaps the whitest of all the white township of Menorca- is a legacy of the French domination (1756-63) during the reign of Louis XV. On its neo-classical church, beneath the shields of the King of France, the Governor (Count de Lannion) and the Intendant (Causán), reads the inscription, "The French dedicated this church to Saint Louis, in the year 1762". The layout of the town follows a strict grid pattern, the main street being directly in line with the due north south Maó road. From this street you will notice two of the windmills so typical of old Menorca**. A number of houses in elegant French style may also be noted. The término of Sant Lluís includes -as well as several look out towers built as a defence against Moorish pirate raids- villages with the special charm of their Menorca-style houses (a number of which have been acquired and converted by English residents), such as Torret and S'Uestra. It also includes the modern "urbanizations" of

Island del Aire

PUNTA PRIMA

BINIBECA

22   *Part of Binibeca*

Binibeca ▲

Binibeca : Landing dock ▼

Binibeca : Landing dock ▼

23

Part of Binibeca

Biniancolla, Punta Prima, Alcaufar, S'Algar, Cap d'en Font, Binisafua and Binibeca, so popular among visitors, so many of whom (and a number of Menorcans, too) have built summer residences there. The last-named includes the recently-built "fishing village" which won its creator a prize and which has become famous throughout the world as a Spanish tourist attraction.

Sant Climent is a pretty agricultural community on the road to Cala'n Porter, beyond the turning to the airport. Administratively it comes under the Ayuntamiento of Maó. It grew bit by bit since the XIV century around a group of peasant dwellings un the region known as Musuptá. The Sant Climent area contains a number of vestiges of the past: before reaching the village itself, but past the airport turning, on the opposite side of the road, a side lane takes you past the talayot known as Torelló and a little further along this lane on the opposite side (just before you reach El Sereno restaurant) may be seen the remains of an old Roman villa or temple (perhaps a paleo-Christian church) with a beautiful mosaic floor, discovered in 1956.

Turning left just on entering the village will take you down a side-road with heavily-grooved surface, flanked by walls with seats for spectators: the reason for this is the trotting races formerly held here. The road continues to the urbanization of Binidalí.

Binibeca

Biniancolla

▲ *Sant Lluís* ▲

Cala Rafalet ▼

▲ *Binissafulla* ▼

Beyond Sant Climent, on the left, is another urbanization, the Sant Climent Golf & Country Club, or Binixica, then another, Son Vitamina, which includes a bar built as a replica of Nelson's flagship, Victory. Off the same turning leads a road to Cales Coves, the site both of some troglodite dwellings (145 in number), in the cliffs overlooking the beautiful double cove, and of a modern urbanization. Finally the main road leads to Cala'n Porter itself, one of the first of all Menorca's urbanizations. All those mentioned in this

Es Canutells ▲

This small statue representing the Egyptian got of medicine, was found at the most important and largest prehistoric talayotic village in the Balearic Islands which is located at Torre d'en Gaumés in Alaior. This site was officially declared an historic artistic monument in 1930. The statue was found while removing a wall from the area surrounding the taula, in 1974.

31

Beach Es Canutells

paragraph are in the término of Maó, with the exception of the last which is in that of Alaior. The town of Alaior may be reached (as well as direct from Maó) by a turning off the Cala'n Porter road which takes you past a taula, or megalithic monument (probably a sacrificial altar) in good state of preservation. It is known as Torrauba d'en Salort. Near it is the impressive well, Na Patarra. The Alaior region must have been a quite highly populated one in ancinet times, to judge by the number of megalithic monuments and Roman roads it contains.

Alaior itself was founded in 1304 by Jaime II of Mallorca. It is conspicuous from all approaches, being densely built on a hill and crowned by its beautiful parish church of Santa Eulalia. Another building worthy of note is the old Fransiscan convent of San Diego, dating from the early XVII century, with its picturesque cloister, Sa Lluna. This and other old parts af Alaior are well worth exploring, as is the nem, well-laidout suburb. The people of Alaior -the Alayorenses- are enterprising: their shoe and furniture industries are well known, as well as their agricultural activities. At the same time they jealously guard their ancient traditions: the feast of San Lorenzo, in mid-August, which is based on a cabalgata, or horse parade, during which the riders go from house and sprinkle the residents with a perfumed water known as aigurrós, supposed to bring them future prosperity, is an example.

Basilica Paleocristiana Son Bou

Beach Son Bou

Torre d'en Gaumés

Sala Hipostila ▼

Cala'n Porter

Beach Cala'n Porter ▲

Airview Cala'n Porter ▼

The Coves of Xoroi

Menorca, ancient highway between East and West, focus of resplendent light in the old Latin sea. Your crystalline tones were like the call of a conch-shell and to you, small and alone, foreign peoples came, but you, noble and pure, wanted to remain Spanish.

Gumersindo Riera

Belvedere from Coves of Xoroi

Menorca made famous by the prodigious skill of your slingers*, whose accurate aim brought you your first laurels, you never wandered from your purpose and now, ever sure of yourself, you still aim your shafts at the target of the heart.

Gumersindo Riera

* The sling was the weapon of megalithic times in the Balearics: in fact the name means the land of the slingers

▲ *Cales Coves* ▼

◄ *Cales Coves* ▲

Troglodyte Coves of Cales Coves ▼

Just beyond Alaior, to the left, a new road leads direct to the beautiful, long sandy beach of Son Bou, at the eastern end of which was recently discovered (in 1951) the remains of a paleo-Christian church dating from the V century. Here, too, is evidence of a troglodite community in the cliff-face caves surrounding the church, the discovery of which led to a controversy in archeological and sub-acua circles on whether or not there was a village now sunk beneath the sea off the Son Bou coast. The remains of this church are now somewhat overshadowed by a multi-storeyed hotel, the first of a number planned for this beach. In the pine-clad hills behind it is the urbanization of San Jaime (which includes a well-designed club-house and restaurant) and further to the westward, on another beach, near a place formerly known as San Adeodato, is the urbanization of Santo Tomás, in the término of Es Mercadal, reached via Es Migjorn Gran.

Es Mercadal itself is at the foot of the island's highest hill, Monte Toro, the name of which, although the same as the Spanish for "bull", is, in fact, a latinization of the Arabic Al-Tor, the mountain. Its summit (wich may

Sa Penya de s'Indio

In your service record, Menorca, you have two days never sufficiently praised: the day of the seige of Barbarroja, which tinged with deepest red the courage of the people of Maó; and some years later, the day when ancient lammona* wove with her blood a crown to palace at your feet.

Gumersindo Riera

* Carthaginian name for Ciutadella

Our island belongs to the sea. She is a prisoner there, with her patron sain of Monte Toro. She is a prisoner there in the prison of the sea, golden shores in turquiose waters.

Gumersindo Riera

be reached by a paved road) has been described as "the balcony of Menorca" and from it you will see the whole of the island spread out beneath you like a vast ship at sea. On it is a beautiful sanctuary built by Augustinian friars in the XVII century and recently restored, where the Virgin (patron saint of the island since the middle ages) is venerated; it is the spiritual centre of Menorca, the scene of many pilgrimages during the spring and summer months, especially on the first Sunday in May, when the Bishop gives his solemn blessing to the Menorcan countryside. There is also a television relay station here.

The término of Es Mercadal includes the urbanizations of Arenal d'en Castell, Na Macaret, Son Parc, Tirant and Binimel.lá on the north coast and Santo Tomas on the south. The bay of Sanitja (used by the Romans) and the whole of the peninsula of Caballería (the most northerly point of the island) are well worth exploring.

The magnificent port of Fornells (pronounced "Fornays"), is 5 km. in length and would rival that of Maó were it deeper. The village itself was formed around the castle of San Antonio (now in ruins) in the XVIII century. It is a peaceful fishing village, the inhabitants of which have now the additional outlets of tourist activities. A visit to Fornells must include a lunch of "caldereta" (lobster soup) and a boat trip to the "Illa de ses Sargantanes", or Lizard Island, where a sub-species of this reptile (unique to the islet) lives.

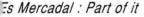
Es Mercadal : Part of it

Es Molí d'es Racó (Es Mercadal)

Court of El Toro

Church sacristia of El Toro

Our woman of El Toro (Saint of Menorca)

Court of El Toro

POSADA

megalithic monument

View of Fornells. In the background Monte Toro

MENORCA

MAÓ

CIUTADELLA

ALAIOR

ES CASTELL

SANT LLUIS

MERCADAL

FERRERIES

ES MIGJORN

Menorca Country Club (Playas de Fornells)

Harbour of Fornells ▲

Cala Pregonda ▼

FORNELLS

Arenal de Son Saura (Son Parc)

Na Macaret

▲ *Aronal d'en Castell* ▼

Harbour of Addaia

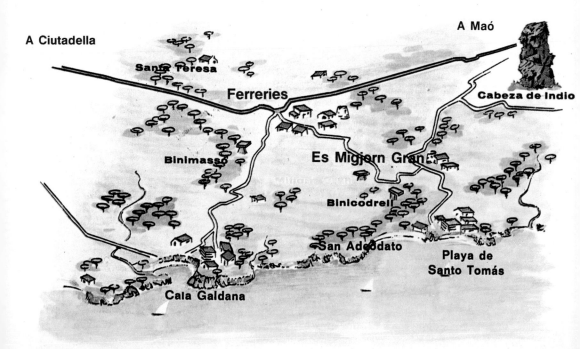

A Ciutadella

A Maó

Santa Teresa

Ferreries

Cabeza de Indio

Binimasso

Es Migjorn Gran

Binicodrell

San Adeodato

Playa de
Santo Tomás

Cala Galdana

Fornells can also be reached direct from Maó. Just after you pass the road leading to Es Grau and the urbanization of Shrangri La, on the opposite side, you will notice the restored monument to Sir Richard Kane and beyond it, on the same side, the beginning of the road which he built across the island.

Es Migjorn Gran, a pleasant village on high ground on the road to Santo Tomás is the large town to the south. It was founded about 1769, as a result of the efforts of a group of men from Ferreries led by one Cristobal Barber, who built a hermitage there. The famous historian of Menorcan folklore and patient student of its customs, stories and songs, Francisco Camps, was born there. The region of Es Migjorn Gran has a greater density of megalithic remains than any in the Balearics: 5 per sq. km., including the great cave of Coloms, as big as a cathedral, the hipostilic hall of Binigaus and the huge talayot of Sant Agustí Vell, the wide chamber of which is unique in Menorcan archeology in having a timbered roof.

62 *Taula de Trepucó*

San Adeodato

Beach Santo Tomás

The name of Ferreries is an obvious clue to its origin: the blacksmith's shop (Herrería in Spanish) which shoed horses beside the main road and provided the nucleus for the growth of the twon. Ferreries now has a spacious modern section with a flourishing forniture industry.

A little further to the west a turning north leads to the mountain Santa Agueda (264 m), reached by a Roman road in fairly good state of preservation. On it are the remains of a fortified castle, Roman in origin but with Moorish towers as well. (One of them is partly overturned, having been dinamitad a few years ago in the erroneous belief that treasure was to be found beneath it). Here it was that the Moors took refuge from Alphonso III in 1287, finally surrendering to him on 21 January of that year.

South of Ferreries is the well know urbanization of Santa Galdana, on one of the most beautiful, pine-clad bays in Menorca. A small river emerges here from a deep barranca, or ravine, which is the boundary between the términos of Ferreries and Ciutadella.

▲ *Part of Galdana* ▼

Detail Cala Galdana ▲

Typical Meal

Beach Cala Galdana

Typical Menorcian shoes (abarcas)

▲ *Part of Cala Galdana* ▶
▼

Arenal de Son Saura. (Ciutadella) ▲

Cala Macarella ▼

▲ *Cala Macarelleta* ▼

ciutadella

Square d'es Born from the harbour ▲

▼ *Town hall of Ciutadella tron the harbour*

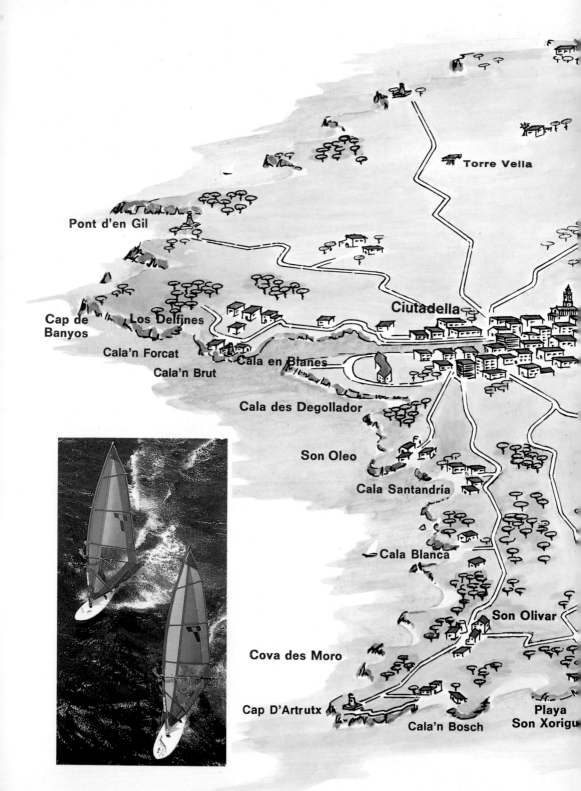

Torre Vella

Pont d'en Gil

Ciutadella

Cap de
Banyos

Los Delfines

Cala'n Forcat

Cala en Blanes

Cala'n Brut

Cala des Degollador

Son Oleo

Cala Santandría

Cala Blanca

Son Olivar

Cova des Moro

Cap D'Artrutx

Cala'n Bosch

Playa
Son Xorigu

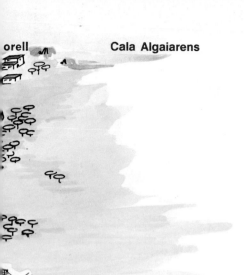

orell Cala Algaiarens

□ Castillo Menorca

A Maó

Torre Llafuda

Naveta des Tudons

Torre Trencada

Sant Joan de Missa

Torre Saura

Cala Turqueta

Cala Macarella

Playa de Son Saura

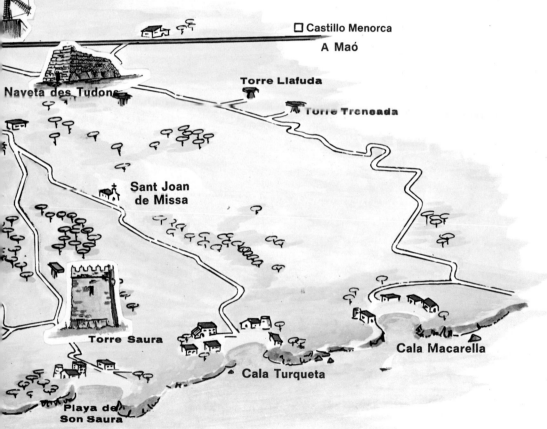

Part of it

CIUTADELLA

An illustrious Ciudadelano, José María Ruiz, a worthy son of the great Menorcan writer mentioned earlier in this little book, has described the town of his birth with photographic exactness:

"If you look at it from the East", he writes, "it resembles a coat-of-arms, a group of houses from which emerges the slim towers of the cathedral and the squat twin towers of the church of San Agustin. Beneath it all the sea. Above, at times, little fleecy clouds seem to hover over the towers. From the South, the town looks like a long ship on its slipway, ready to be launched, new and heroic despite the centuries. From the West it is the proud city that has lived through times of war behind its stone walls. But from the North it is Jerusalem itself. The wall is brown in this part, the domes and the churches white as lime. Two erect palm trees are motionless as in pictures from the Bible ..."

Ciutadella can be reached from two principal directions: from Maó by the main road, or from the sea. The main road, after passing Sa Naveta d'es Tudons ("the oldest building in Europe") on the left, soon becomes a tree-lined approach to the city. From the sea you enter by the long and narrow port of Ciutadella. In the XVII century an octagonal tower was built to protect the entrance to this port. Near it, now, may be seen the monument to the first admiral of the U.S. Navy, David Farragut, son of a Ciudadelano.

Ciutadella harbour

Ses Voltes. Part of it

Ciutadella. Part of square d'es Born

The whole island is a passionate kiss; a song which invites me to sing; love which responds to my yearnings for love.

A sweet secret nestles in the island's heart; love made of life and the sleep. For the island treasures the secret of loving. The island is a woman: that is the secret of her enchantment.

Love, love, you may come and go, but while you come and go your heart will remain in this enchanted island, lost in the middle of the sea.

Gumersindo Riera

It is worth taking a look at the old port and its picturesque features: the ancient fishermen's houses with their external staircases, the fishing nets drying in the sun, the quayside taverns from which emerge the sounds of strumming guitars and voices in song: the arrival of the fishing boats, all the colours of the rainbow scintillating from the scales of their catch. And in the tourist season, "snipes" and yachts with flags of all nationalities moored cheek by jowl.

Entrance Ciutadella harbour

Cathidral Menorca. Ciutadella

Walking up to the city from the port we find ourselves in a large square surrounded by buildings of noble architecture, some with neo-classical arcades and (a modern touch) two illuminated fountains. At one end, looking over the port, is the Casa Consistorial (town hall), built on the site formerly occupied by the Real Alcázar (royal castle) used as a residence by the conqueror of Menorca, Alphonso III, and later as the Governor's Palace, when Ciutadella was the capital of the island, i.e. until 1722, during the British occupation, when Sir Richard Kane ordered the capital to be transferred to Maó. This square is called the Born, a word meaning palisade, an enclosure made with piles, because it was here that the noblemen of old held their tournaments and other equestrian contests.

In 1558 Ciutadella withstood a nine-day seige against 15,000 Turks, who finally assaulted the city and, in the course of the next three days, destroyed it almost completely and took what few survivors remained as captives to Constantinople. So great was the destruction that the new, provisional

Ses Voltes (Ciutadella)

governor had to spend his first night of office in a cave, as there was no house standing. The obelisk in the centre of the square commemorates that tragic event and bears four inscriptions in Latin, (work of the great Ciudadelan poligraphist, José María Quadrado), reading. "Here we fought until death, for our religion and our country, in the year 1558". The bastions of La Fuente and Puerto and the sea wall itself are now the sole remains of the old city wall, which had five gateways and which defended the city in ancient times. (The avenues of Negrete, Conquistador and José Antonio follow its ancient route).

Inside Sa Naveta : 1º and 2 floor

Sa Naveta d'es Tudons

Entrance Ciutadella harbour ▲

Cala'n Blanes ▼

Airview H. Almirante Farragut. Cala'n Blanes

As well as these reminders of a past both martial and heroic the ancient Menorcan capital contains many aristocratic palaces which give it its characteristic appearance. Towards the end of the XVI century the knights to whom the king had given small fiefdoms as a mark of his favour, came to live in Ciutadella. These fiefdoms (or "cavalleries", as they were called) were granted by the king with the intention of turning their holders, with their fortified towers, their war horses and bands of armed men, into a loyal defense force, ever at the ready to repel the frequent incursions of Moorish raiders. Later on, these knights, resident in Ciutadella, built up and enlarged their ancestral homes, converting them into real palaces, of which the most outstanding is perhaps that of the Counts of Torre Saura, on the Born itself, which bears the date of 1697. Externally, these mansions are of many different styles. Inside (if you can get yourself invited, often more difficult than crossing the Calatrava!) your eyes will feast on a real museum of antique furniture, family portraits of the XVII and XVIII centuries, historic costumes, English etchings and water colours by the famous Italian painter, Giuseppe Chiesa. The gardens of these lordly mansions are interesting, too, with their melancholy, evocative of a life hardly imaginable to our modern minds.

Pont d'en Gil

Ciutadella has been the episcopal see of Menorca since the re-establishment there of the old bishopric which had existed since the XV century. The Cathedral is a fine, Gothic structure, commenced towards the end of of the XIII century and completed about 1362. It has a single, wide nave, six chapels on each side and a pentagonal apse. The neo-classical façade of the west front is in rather unhappy contrast with the style of the church itself. Restored after the Civil War of 1936-39 it was honoured with the title of Basilica in 1953. Other religious buildings of note are the old Augustinian convent of Socós, (later a seminary and the Bishop's palace), adjoining the cathedral, with its cloistered garden and monolithic cistern-head, forming one of the most beautiful and secluded spots in Ciutadella; the church of San Francisco, in which the late Gothic of the nave blends with the neo-classic of the transept and dome; the old church of Rosario, with its baroque façade; and the little renaissance church of Santo Cristo. The tortuous old streets of Ciutadella, their houses with small, asymmetrical windows, thick, whitewashed walls of natural stone, low, timbered roofs, are Moorish in appearance. The arcades of Calle José María Quadrado and Plaza de España are particularly noteworty and famous.

CALA'N BOSCH

Ciutadella, with its roots deep in the traditions of its past, nevertheless has an eye to the future. Ever since Jerónimo Cabrisas established here, round about 1853, the luxury shoe trade, the general economic level of the inhabitants has improved greatly. Men and women work in this industry, as also in jewelry and other light industries. Ciutadella is undoubtedly a city of contrasts.

This contrast, or rather harmonious symbiosis, between the heroic, aristocratic past and the modern zest for enjoyment, is given ceremonious expression every year on the feast of San Juan (June 23), with ist cavalcade of richly-caparisoned horses led by a flag of the Order of Malta and presided over by representatives of the nobility, the church and the people. It is a ceremony without a programme. No one needs one, it is all based on tradition. It is followed, as in the feast-days of all Menorca towns, by a general "Jaleo", when prancing horses mix with the crowd, while laughing youths rush between their legs trying to unseat their riders, all to the music of pipe and tambourine.

The término of Ciutadella includes a number of urbanitations, such as Morell, Cala'n Blanes, Santandria, Cala Blanca, Cap d'Artruitx.

A BRIEF LOOK AT MENORCA'S HISTORY

It is difficult to summarise in a few lines the past of an island which, albeit small in physical size, has so much of historical interest that, to quote the words of the writer Mario Verdaguer, "not even the furious onslaughts of the Tramontana could cut through it".

The very situation of Menorca made it the cross-roads of the various political and cultural forces which have spread throughout the Mediterranean since the most ancient times. Hence any account of Menorca's past must begin with ist pre-history. The island is so strewn with megalithic remains as to make it a vast open-air museum. Following the ancient cave culture, an age of splendour must have developed in the bronze age, to judge by the profusion of cyclopean* construction: talayots, navetas, taulas, hipostilic halls, walls and covered galleries. Later on, Phoenecian and Greek traders left marks of their visits and later still the Carthaginians conquered the island and founded the towns of Magón, or Maguén (Maó) and Jamma (Ciutadella), probably on the sites of prehistoric villages; remains of other such villages may be seen at Torre d'en Gaumes (Alaior), Trepucó (Maó), Son Catllar and Torre Vella (Cuitadella).

The Romans conquered the Balearics in 123 B.C. They gave Menorca the origin of its present name: Balearics Minor, or Minorica, as distinct from Balearics Mayor, Mallorca. The Roman capital was Magona (Maó), or, to give it its full title, Municipio Flavio Magontano. Jamma (Ciutadella) became lamona and Pliny refers to another town, Sanisera, later Sanitja, the bay to which we have already referred. The Romans built about 20 roads on the island and left a number of archeologial remains.

*Term used to denote the characteristic dry walls of large stones, often in-filled whith small ones; first used by Greeks, who thought only the race of one-eyed giants could lift such stones.

Cala Blanca

Cala'n Bosch

Christianity reached Menorca early. The famous latter of Bishop Severo, written in 417, gives a minute description of an already flourishing Menorcan church. The various churches which have been discovered show that there were Christian places of worship not only in the towns but out in the country and beside the sea.

The Romans were displaced by the Vandals, whose conquests spread from the Beotic peninsular to the Balearics and North Africa. In 484 the Bishop of Menorca, Macario, was obliged to stand up for his faith to the Arian king Hunnericus, a great persecutor of Christians. Then the vandals were defeated by the Byzantine Empire and there was peace in the island for a while, until, after repeated raids by the Moors, already masters of the whole of Spain, the Balearics were occupied in about 913 and became subject to the Caliphate of Córdoba. With the break-up of the Caliphate, the islands passed into the sovereignity if the king of Denia, then of Mallorca, until finally Menorca was the only Muslim territory in eastern Spain, as other parts fell into the hands of Christian conquerors.

Jaleo. Typica Menorcian feast

Each festival in Menorca is a way to measure time. After they have finished, people already dream of the next one and start to prepare the following year's. Our traditional festivals, in which horses and riders are their tru protagonists, are a means of social communication, as well as an act of respect, of reaffirmation in the own origins.

Protocols and costumes are mixed together, while the horses, beautifully harnessed, jump among people's joy and the riders - "caixers"-, while making a show of their skills, greet joyfully the people while they hold the bridle of their fiery mounts.

Sant Joan in Ciutadella conserves protocols and tradition of its unique, incomparable festivals to the highest degree.

Riding demostration

Queso Mahón

Cheese Mahón. Original denomination

In 1232 Jaime I of Aragón, by dint of the trick of lighting a large number of fires in the region of Capdepera, Mallorca, led the Muslin chief of Menorca to believe he had a large army prepared to conquer that island and thus induced him to become a tributary to the crown of Aragón. But a later Menorcan chief was guilty of betraying the Aragón king, Pedro III, to avenge which, his son, Alphonso III, having already taken Mallorca from his uncle, Jaime II, set about conquering Menorca. This he achieved in January 1287. Under the treaty of Anagui the Balearics were returned to Jaime II of Mallorca, who worked effectively for the good government of Menorca: he granted that island a Peoples' Charter and divided up the land in a more equitable manner than that of his predecessor and nephew, Alphonso III, after the conquest: he founded the town of Alaior and established the island's parochial system. After the defeat of the last king of Mallorca at Llucmajor in 1343 the Balearics were finally incorporated into the kingdom of Aragón by Pedro IV.

In 1535 the Turkish pirate Barbarroja devastated Maó with slaughter and pillage and took thousands captive. (Even greater was the misfortune which befell Ciutadella in 1558, as related in the previous chapter).

The XVII century was particularly disastrous for the island. As well as the constant danger of invasion by Muslim pirates or by the European enemies of Spain, there were droughts, plagues of crop pests and acts of violence committed by bandits -who on one occasion, in 1636, killed the governor himself, don Juan Valenciano de Mendiolaza- and a cholera epidemic which decimated Ciutadella from April 1652 until the end of the following year. At the beginning of the XVIII century the English, having beem called in to support the Austrian (Carlist) claim in the War of the Spanish Succession, took Menorca and decided to keep it for themselves. This was in 1708. In 1713 this situation was ratified by the Treaty of Utrecht and English rule lasted until 1756, Sir Richard Kane being a particularly outstanding governor. In 1756 French troops, under the command of Marshal the Duke of Richelieu, landed just south of Ciutadella, marched across the island to the fortress of San Felipe, where the British forces, because of the regretable affair of Admiral Byng, were obligated to surrender after a long seige. The French remained until 1763 when, by the Treaty of París, they returned the island to Great Britain. The second British domination lasted until 1782 when the fort of San Felipe, in which they were holding out, again fell, this time as a result of direct assault by combined Franco-Spanish forces under the Duke of Crillón. During the brief period of Spanish rule which followed (1782-98) it is not surprising that this fortress, originally constructed in the early XVI century as a defence against Moorish invasion and believed even by the Duke of Richelieu to be impregnable, was destroyed, by the Spanish themselves in 1782. The British again conquered the island, in 1798 and remained for four years until, in 1802, by the Treaty of Amiens, Menorca reverted finally to Spain.

The British occupations had brought prosperity to the island and, with the economic decline which succeeded them, Menorcan emigration to the New World (particularly Florida and California) grew and continued throughout the XIX and present centuries. In 1830 Menorcans colonised a number of places in Algeria, especially Font d'Eau. But at the same time the foundation of new industries and urban improvements paved the way for subsequent prosperity, which, despite the tragic set-back of the Civil War, continues to grow, aided by the influx of tourists who no doubt bring to Menorca, as well as affluence, socio-economic influences the significance of which we cannot yet know.

Ciutadella. Beach Algaiarens

Typical gates

HOTELS OF MENORCA

HOTELS 4 STARS ★★★★

Open Months	Name and Direction	Rooms	Beds
4-10	AUDAX, tel. 37 31 25 Cala Galdana - Ferreries	244	458
1-12	PORT-MAHON tel. 36 26 00 Avda. Fort de L'eau s/n - Maó	74	140
4-10	SANTO TOMAS, tel. 37 00 25 Sant Tomàs - Es Migjorn	60	114

HOTEL-APARTMENT ★★★★

Open Months	Name and Direction	Rooms	Beds
5-10	LAS MARISMAS, tel. 37 80 40 Torre Soli. Alaior	288	
5-10	SAN VALENTIN, tel. 37 29 56 Urb. Torre Solí - Alaior	312	652

HOTELS 3 STARS ★★★

Open Months	Name and Direction	Rooms	Beds
4-10	AGAMENON, tel. 36 21 50 Paratge Fontanillas - Es Castell	75	140
4-10	AGUAMARINA, tel. 37 98 17 Arenal d'en Castell - Es Mercadal	248	468
5-10	ALMIRANTE FARRAGUT, tel. 38 28 00 Cala'n Forcat - Ciutadella	472	880
4-10	CALA BLANCA, tel. 38 04 50 Cala Blanca - Ciutadella	148	281
4-10	CALA GALDANA, tel. 37 30 00 Cala Galdana. Ferrerías	259	580
5-10	CALA'N BOSCH, tel. 38 06 00 Cala'n Bosch - Ciutadella	170	320
4-10	CASTELL PLAYA, tel. 37 99 09 Arenal d'en Castell - Es Mercadal	264	501
4-10	CLUB FALCO, tel. 38 46 23 Urb. Son Xoriguer - Ciutadella	450	855
4-10	ESMERALDA, tel. 38 02 50 Passeig Sant Nicolau - Ciutadella	135	252
1-12	HAMILTON, tel 36 20 50 Passeig Sta. Agueda, 6 - Es Castell	132	248
5-10	LORD NELSON tel. 37 01 25 Sant Tomàs - Es Migjorn	177	340
4-10	LOS CONDORES, tel. 37 00 50 Sant Tomàs - Es Migjorn	184	352
4-10	LOS GAVILANES tel. 37 31 75 Cala Galdana - Ferreríes	357	679
4-10	LOS MILANOS, tel. 37 11 75 Son Bou - Alaior	300	570
4-10	LOS PINGUINOS, tel. 37 10 75 Son Bou - Alaior	300	570
4-10	MEDITERRANI, tel. 38 42 03 Urb. Cala Blanca - Ciutadella	180	342
1-12	MIRADOR DES PORT, tel. 35 28 68 C/ Vilanova, 1. Maó	70	133
1-12	PRINSHOTEL - LA CALETA. 38 23 99 Caleta Santandría - Ciutadella	247	421
4-10	REY CARLOS III, tel. 36 31 00 Miranda Cala Corp - Es Castell	87	157
1-12	SAGITARIO, tel. 38 28 77 Urb. Cala Blanca - Ciutadella	72	132

Open Months	Name and Direction	Rooms	Beds
3-10	S'ALGAR, tel. 15 17 00 Urb. S'Algar - Sant Lluís	106	204
5-10	SAN LUIS, tel. 15 17 50 Urb. S'Algar - Sant Lluís	228	434
	VICTORIA PLAYA, tel. 37 02 00 Sant Tomás - Es Migjorn	266	505

HOTEL-APARTMENT ★★★

4-10	MAR DE MENORCA, tel. 15 30 95 Urb. Cala Canutells - Maó	278	1.140
5-10	MENORCA STARS, tel. 38 57 64 - 38 58 85 Urb. Cala'n Bosch - Ciutadella	143	404
5-10	ROYAL SON BOU, tel. 37 23 58 Son Bou - Alaior	252	504

HOTEL-RESIDENCE 3 STARS ★★★

1-12	CAPRI, tel. 36 14 00 C/ Sant Esteve, 8, Maó	75	140
1-12	PATRICIA tel. 38 55 11 P.º San Nicolás, 90. Ciutadella	70	133

RESIDENCE-APARTMENT 3 STARS ★★★

5-10	LORD NELSON, tel. 37 02 25 Urb. Sant Tomás - Es Migjorn	143	286
	SOL DEL ESTE MAR, tel. 36 90 84 - 36 80 10 Urb. Sol del Este - Es Castell	96	259

HOLIDAYS CITY

5-10	CALIMERA, tel. 38 05 50 Urb. Cala'n Bosch - Ciutadella	220	880

HOTEL 2 STARS ★★

5-10	CALA'N BLANES, tel. 38 24 97 Cala'n Blanes - Ciutadella	103	188
5-10	POSEIDON, tel. 38 26 44 Santandría - Ciutadella	13	24
4-10	SES VOLTES, tel. 38 04 00 Santandría - Ciutadella	40	77
4-10	TOPACIO, tel. 37 98 34 Arenal d'en Castell - Es Mercadal	276	516

RESIDENCIE-APARTMENT 2 STARS ★★

1-12	LOAR tel. 37 41 81 Reverendo Padre Huguet, 1 - Ferreries	30	
5-10	SOL PARC, tel. 37 66 45 Urb. Son Parc, Es Mercadal	272	816
5-10	BEACH CLUB tel. 37 67 15 Urb. Son Parc - Es Mercadal	196	588

HOTEL 1 STAR ★

1-12	ALFONSO III tel. 38 01 50 Camí de Maó, 53. Ciutadella	52	82
4-10	AQUARIUM tel. 37 70 00 Cala'n Porter - Alaior	59	112
5-10	DEL ALMIRANTE tel. 36 27 00 Ctra. Maó - Es Castell	38	76
4-10	PLAYA AZUL tel. 37 71 25 Cala'n Porter - Alaior	124	237

Open Months	Name and Direction	Rooms	Beds
4-10	PUEBLO MENORCA tel. 15 18 50	538	1.104
	Punta Prima - Sant Lluís		
5-10	SA BARRERA tel. 37 71 26	23	44
	Cala'n Porter - Alaior		
4-10	SUR MENORCA tel. 15 18 00	239	506
	Biniancolla - Sant Lluís		
5-10	XALOC tel. 15 01 06	58	124
	Punta Prima - Sant Lluís		

HOTEL RESIDENCE 2 STARS ★★

5-10	LOS DELFINES tel. 38 24 50	95	179
	Urb. Los Delfines. Ciutadella		

HOTEL RESIDENCE 1 STAR ★

4-9	CALA BONA tel. 38 00 16	16	29
	Son Oleo - Ciutadella		
	GEMINIS tel. 38 58 96	19	36
	C/ Josefa Rossinyol, s/n. Ciutadella		

HOSTELRY 3 STARS ★★★

4-10	BINIALI tel. 15 17 24	9	21
	Ctra. S'Uestrà - Sant Lluís		
	IRIS, tel. 37 63 92	17	32
	C/ Major, 17 - Fornells		

HOSTELRY 2 STARS ★★

1-12	DANIEL'S tel. 38 42 31	16	28
	Camí de Maó, 178. Ciutadella		
4-9	MAR BLAVA tel. 38 00 16	18	36
	Urb. Son Oleo - Ciutadella		
5-10	S'ALGARET tel. 37 66 74	23	46
	S'algaret, 7 - Fornells		
5-10	SON ROSSINYOL tel. 15 11 06	18	36
	Ctra. Binibeca - Sant Lluis		
5-10	XUROY tel. 15 18 20	44	87
	Alcaufar - Sant Lluis		

HOSTELRY-RESIDENCE 2 STARS ★★

1-12	CIUTADELLA tel. 38 34 62	17	39
	Sant Eloi, 10 - Ciutadella		
1-12	NOA tel. 36 12 00	40	68
	Cos de Gracia, 157 - Maó		
1-12	MENURKA tel. 38 14 15	21	34
	C/ Fred, 6 - Ciutadella		
5-10	MIRAMAR tel. 36 29 00	30	57
	Fonduco - Es Castell		
4-10	PORT-FORNELLS Tel. 37 63 73	20	39
	Ses Salines - Fornells		

HOSTELRY 1 STAR ★

5-10	CASTILLO SANCHO PANZA tel. 37 73 84	18	31
	Cala'n Porter. Alaior		
1-12	HORIZONTE tel. 36 29 22	16	31
	Plaça Horizonte - Es Castell		
1-12	LA ISLA tel. 36 64 92	15	24
	Santa Caterina, 4 - Maó		
1-12	MADRID tel. 38 03 28	11	22
	C/ Madrid, s/n - Ciutadella		
4-10	MAR BLAVA	30	49
	Platja Punta Prima - Sant Lluís		

Open Months	Name and Direction	Rooms	Beds
1-12	OASIS tel. 38 21 97	9	18
	Sant Isidre, 33 - Ciutadella		
5-9	PUNTA PRIMA	25	39
	Platja Punta Prima - Sant Lluís		
1-12	REYNES tel. 36 40 59	27	45
	C/ Comerç, 6 - Maó		
1-12	SA PRENSA tel. 38 26 98	4	8
	Plaça Madrid, s/n - Ciutadella		
1-12	SHEILA tel. 36 48 55	12	24
	Santa Cecilia, 41 - Maó		

HOSTELRY-RESIDENCE 1 STAR ★

Open Months	Name and Direction	Rooms	Beds
4-10	CLUB MENORCA tel. 37 71 59	28	48
	Cala'n Porter - Alaior		
1-12	JENI tel. 37 50 59	22	44
	Miranda del Toro, 81 - Es Mercadal		
1-12	JUME tel. 36 32 66	35	65
	C/ Concepción, 6 - Maó		
1-12	LA PERDIZ tel. 37 30 48	27	48
	C/ Maó, 14 - Ferreries		
1-12	ORSI tel. 36 47 51	16	26
	C/ Infanta, 19 - Maó		
1-12	PARIS tel. 38 16 22	13	20
	Ctra. Santandría, s/n - Ciutadella		
1-12	ROCA tel. 35 08 39	14	26
	C/ Carmen, 37 - Maó		
5-10	ROCAMAR tel. 36 56 01	21	42
	Fonduco, 32 - Es Castell		
5-10	SA PAYSA tel. 37 73 89	26	48
	Cala'n Porter - Alaior		
1-12	SA ROQUETA tel. 36 43 35	22	39
	C/ Carmen, 122 - Maó		
1-12	TONI tel. 36 59 99	13	19
	C/ Castillo, 3 - Es Castell		

INN

Open Months	Name and Direction	Rooms	Beds
	NORAY tel. 15 10 71	18	26
	Platja Punta Prima - Sant Lluís		
	OAR tel. 37 38 88	10	15
	C/ Verge de Monte Toro, 2 - Ferreríes		
	PLAYA GRANDE tel. 38 07 93	20	34
	C/ Bisbe Juano, 4 - Ciutadella		
	S'ENGOLIDOR tel. 37 01 93	4	7
	C/ 8 de Febrer, 58 - Es Migjorn		

BOARDING HOUSE

Open Months	Name and Direction	Rooms	Beds
	COMPANY tel. 36 22 67	7	11
	C/ Rosari, 27 - Maó		
	ESPAÑA tel. 38 02 88	10	14
	Camí de Maó, 13 - Ciutadella		
	ESPAÑA tel. 36 36 86	9	16
	Camí d'es Castell, 205 - Maó		
	LA PALMA tel. 37 66 34	17	30
	S'algaret, 3 - Fornells		
	LA PALMERA tel. 37 00 23	14	23
	Plaça Generalíssim, 19 - Es Migjorn		
	LAS PERSIANAS tel. 38 14 45	8	16
	Plaça d'Artruitx, 2 Ciutadella		
	VALLDEMOSA tel. 38 07 00	14	22
	República Argentina, 84 - Ciutadella		

TOURING APARTMENT OF MENORCA

TERMINO OF MAÓ

Name and Direction	Rooms	Ct.
CASA MARGARITA. C/ Mártires de Atlante, 71	16	3ª
ROYAL. C/ del Carmen, 131. Tel 36 95 34	102	3ª
BINI-DALI. Urb. Binidali. San Clemente. Tel. 15 09 91	72	3ª

TERMINO OF SANT LLUIS

Name and Direction	Rooms	Ct.
AMSTERDAM. Playa Binisafua	8	3ª
BIENVENIDO. Playa Binisafua	60	3ª
BINICUDI. Urb. Binibeca Vell	100	3ª
BINIFUM. Urb. Binibeca Vell	24	3ª
BINIVELL. Urb. Binibeca Vell (Pueblo de Pescadores). Tel. 15 06 08	321	2ª
BINIBECA CLUB. Urb. Binisafua. Tel. 15 06 08		1ª
BOYERA, LA. Urb. Binisafua. Tel. 15 17 86	66	2ª
COMPLEJO PISCINA BINISAFUA. Playa Binisafua. Tel. 15 18 67	41	2ª
CHUMBERAS, LAS. Urb. Binibeca Vell. Tel. 36 01 84	28	3ª
DOLCE VITA. Cala Alcaufar. Tel. 15 18 20	20	3ª
JARDIN. Urb. S'Algar. Tel. 15 17 62	80	2ª
MENORCA. Urb. S'Algar. Tel. 15 17 62	30	3ª
NARANJOS, LOS. Urb. S'Algar. Tel. 15 17 62	220	1ª
PALMERAS, LAS. Urb. S'Algar. Tel. 15 17 61	216	2ª
PETIT XUROY. Cala Alcaufar. Tel. 15 18 20	33	3ª
PUEBLO CALA TORRET. Urb. Binibeca. Cala Toret. Tel. 15 16 18 - 17 99	532	3ª
RAFALET. Urb. S'Algar. Tel 15 17 62	100	1ª
SON GANXO, Urb. Son Ganxo. Parc, 116	31	3ª
VISTA FARO. Urb. S'Algar. Tel. 15 17 62	132	2ª

TERMINO OF ES MERCADAL

Name and Direction	Rooms	Ct.
ALDEA COUNTRY CLUB. Playas de Fornells	271	2ª
ALBATROS. Urb. Punta Grossa, Parc, 107	33	3ª
ARCO IRIS. Urb. Punta Grossa	25	2ª
ARENAL PLAYA. Urb. Arenal d'en Castell	36	2ª
AREPAR. Urb. Arenal d'en Castell	120	2ª
BELISAS I, LAS. Urb. Punta Grossa. Parc, 73-74. Tel. 37 13 21	44	3ª
BELISAS II, LAS. Urb. Punta Grossa. Parc, 105. Tel. 37 13 21	32	3ª
CAN DIGUS. C/ Viveros, s/n. Fornells. Tel. 37 64 11 - 66 16	54	2ª
CASTELLSOL. Urb. Arenal d'en Castell	112	3ª
ELS ESTELS. Urb. Son Parc. Parc, 24, 25, 26	240	3ª
ELS VENTS. Urb. Son.Parc. Parc, 15 y 16	138	3ª
JARDIN PLAYA. Urb. Arenal d'en Castell	18	2ª
FORNELLS. C/ J. Antonio, 21. Fornells	22	3ª
PERELLO CARRERAS I. Urb. Ses Salines, 14. Fornells	48	3ª
PERELLO CARRERAS II. Urb. Ses Salines, 24. Fornells	20	3ª
ROCAS MARINAS. Urb. Punta Grossa	40	3ª
PERGOLAS, LAS. Urb. Son Parc. Parc, 22	80	3ª
SES CASETES DE S'ARENAL. Urb. Arenal d'en Castell	36	3ª
SOL ISLA I. Urb. Arenal d'en Castell	270	3ª
SOL ISLA II. Urb. Arenal d'en Castell	240	3ª
TORRALBA. Urb. Punta Grossa. Parc, 104	24	3ª

TERMINO OF ES MIGJORN GRAN

Name and Direction	Rooms	Ct.
AGRYTURSA. Urb. Santo Tomás. Tel. 37 00 79	40	2ª
HAMILTON COURT. Urb. Santo Tomás. Tel. 37 00 86	528	2ª
LLEBEIG. Urb. Santo Tomás. Tel. 37 03 46 - 03 70	300	2ª
MESTRAL. Urb. Santo Tomás. Tel. 37 03 46 - 03 70	354	2ª
MIGJORN. Urb. Santo Tomás. C/ Principal. Tel. 37 00 79	67	3ª
PLAYA SANTO TOMAS. Playa Santo Tomás. Tel. 37 00 79	38	1ª
VISTAMAR. Urb. Santo Tomás	150	2ª

TERMINO OF FERRERIES

CALA GALDANA. Urb. Cala Galdana	20	3ª
EL RIO. Urb. Cala Galdana	30	3ª

TERMINO OF ALAIOR

ALBAIDA. Urb. Torre Solí Nou, E-1. Tel. 36 04 00	80	1ª
BAHIA PARK I. Urb Calan Porter. Tel. 37 70 88	150	2ª
C.H. CALAN PORTER. C/ Tramontana, Manzana ch. Urb. Calan Porter. Tel. 36 10 50	64	3ª
CALA, LA. C/ Sa Barrera, 4. Urb. Calan Porter	27	2ª
CALAN PORTER. C/ Tramontana, 3, 4 y 5. Urb. Calan Porter	180	2ª
CONSEY I. Urb. Calan Porter	24	3ª
COSTA ARENAL. Urb. Arenal d'en Castell (B1-A2)	384	3ª
ELS GIRASOLS. Urb. San Jaime Mediterráneo. ZEH-6	264	2ª
ISABEL. C/ Iglesia 8 y 9. Urb. Calan Porter	11	3ª
J-9. C/ Mediterráneo. Urb. Calan Porter . Tel. 36 04 44	16	2ª
JUAN. C/ Xaloc y Tramontana. Urb. Calan Porter. Tel. 37 18 21	9	3ª
MASIN. Urb. San Jaime Mediterráneo ZEH- del 45 al 56	48	3ª
MASIN II. Urb. San Jaime Mediterráneo	32	3ª
SAN JAIME I. Urb. San Jaime ZEH3. Tel. 37 20 00	212	2ª
SAN JAIME II. Urb. San Jaime ZEH3 y 4. Tel. 37 20 00	182	2ª
SAN JAIME III. Urb. San Jaime ZEH-5. Tel. 37 20 00	440	3ª
SAN JAIME ECHEZARRETA. Urb. San Jaime	16	3ª
SAN JAIME MINORICA. Urb. San Jaime Mediterráneo	32	3ª
SIESTAMAR A, B. Urb. Calan Porter. Parc, M. Av. Central. Tel. 37 74 06	132	2ª
SIESTAMAR, C. Urb. Calan Porter. Parc, M. Av. Central. Tel. 37 74 06	50	3ª
SIESTAMAR II. Urb. Calan Porter. Tel. 37 74 06	153	2ª
SOL Y MAR. C/ Migjorn. Urb. Calan Porter	24	2ª
SON BOU. Urb. San Jaime. Parc, 47-48	30	3ª
SUPERMERCADO. Avda. Central. Urb. Calan Porter	15	3ª
TOM. C/ Tramontana. Urb. Calan Porter	9	3ª

TERMINO OF CIUTADELLA

ALDEA CALA'N BOSCH. Urb. Son Xoriguer, s/n. Tel. 38 62 11	256	2ª
ALDEA III. Urb. Cap D'Artruix, 15-A. Tel. 38 08 49	42	2ª
ALONDRAS, LAS. Urb. Torre del Ram	18	3ª
ALTA GALDANA. Urb. Serpentona	105	3ª
AUDAX BEACH. Urb. Serpentona. Tel. 38 00 28	100	3ª
AN-MAR. Urb. Cales Piques. Parc, 402	60	3ª
ANNABELS. Urb. Serpentona, 33	25	3ª
AUGUST I. Urb. Cala Blanca, 151-152	24	3ª
AUGUST II. Urb. Cala Blanca, 179-180	12	3ª
AUGUST III. Urb. Cala Blanca, 169-170	9	3ª
BINICEL BLAU. Urb. Tamarinda. Tel. 38 02 52	42	3ª
BINIFORCAT. Urb. Los Delfines	200	2ª
BINILAFER I. Urb. Cala Blanca, 8	40	3ª
BINILAFER II. Urb. Cala Piques, 412	24	2ª

Name and Direction	Rooms	Ct.
BINIMART. Urb. Cala Piques, D.	808	2ª
BLANCALA. Urb. Blanca Cala. Tel. 38 64 01	80	2ª
BOLIVIA. Urb. Son Carrió	56	3ª
BON REPÒS. Urb. Cala'n Bosch. Tel. 38 17 00 - 14 63	27	3ª
BRISAS I, LAS. Urb. Son Xoriguer	48	3ª
BRISAS II, LAS. Urb Son Xoriguer	48	3ª
BUGANVILLAS. Urb. Los Delfines	36	3ª
CALA BLANCA. Urb. Cala Blanca	56	3ª
CALA'N BLANES. Urb. Cala'n Blanes	36	2ª
CALA'N BLANES BUNGALOWS. Urb. Cala'n Blanes	140	3ª
CALA GALDANA PLAYA. Urb. Serpentona	84	3ª
CALA FORCAT. Urb. Los Delfines	72	3ª
CALA PIQUES. Urb. Los Delfines . Tel. 38 21 69	56	3ª
CALETA, LA. Urb. Sa Caleta. Tel. 38 16 81	32	3ª
CALETA PLAYA. Urb. Sa Caleta, F-16	93	3ª
CALIFORNIA I. Urb. Torre del Ram. Pol. 1. Tel. 38 13 75	31	3ª
CALIFORNIA II. Urb. Torre del Ram. Pol, 1 . Tel. 38 13 75	28	3ª
CAMPS. Urb. Torre del Ram. Tel. 38 34 19	32	3ª
CATALÀ RIERA. Urb. Sa Caleta	36	3ª
CEL BLAU. Cap D'Artruix, 13-A	30	3ª
CISNE BLANCO, EL. Urb. Torre del Ram. Parc. 7	30	2ª
CLUB ANDRIA. Urb. Son Carrió, 114 a 118. Tel. 38 48 81	168	3ª
CLUB MENORCA. Urb. Son Xoriguer. Tel. 38 00 98	406	2ª
CONFORT. Urb. Serpentona	45	2ª
COLL CARRERAS. Urb. San Caleta. Parc, 15	36	3ª
DELFIMAR. Urb. Los Delfines. Tel. 38 21 75	96	2ª
DELFINES CLUB, LOS. Urb. Torre del Ram II	244	2ª
DESMAIS. Urb. Serpentona	60	2ª
DIANA. Urb. Torre del Ram. 7, 8, 19 y 20	80	2ª
DIONI. Urb. Son Xoriguer, B-37, B-55	40	3ª
DUNA. Urb. Cala Blanca, 265	9	3ª
DUNAS, LAS. Urb. Son Xoriguer, 68. Tel. 38 49 51	24	3ª
ENTREPLAYAS I. Urb. Son Xoriguer	35	2ª
ENTREPLAYAS II. Urb. Son Xoriguer	70	3ª
ES FUMERALS. C/ San Nicolás, 133. Ciutadella	82	3ª
EUGENIA. Urb. Torre del Ram. Tel. 38 01 18	25	3ª
FLORA PARK. Urb. Calan Bosch	188	2ª
GOLONDRINAS, LAS. Urb. Calan Bosch	80	3ª
GAZANIAS. Urb. Los Delfines 12 y 13	12	3º
INTER. Urb. Cala Blanca, 17	43	3ª
JUANI. Urb. Serpentona, parc, 19	20	3ª
LANTANAS, LAS. Urb. Los Delfines. Tel. 38 12 93	30	3ª
LENTISCOS, LOS. Urb. Los Delfines. Tel. 38 40 06	360	2ª
LLEBEIG. Urb. Son Carrió. Tel. 38 42 47	24	3ª
MAR BLANCA. Urb. Cala Blanca	72	3ª
MAR Y MAR. Urb. Torre del Ram	22	3ª
MARIBEL. Urb. Cala Blanca, 104-A	32	3ª
MARIBEL AVENIDA. Urb. Cala Blanca. Pol. B. 1-E	30	2ª
MARIBEL III. Urb. Cala Blanca, Pol. A, P-33/60	45	3ª
MARINA I. Urb. Cala'n Bosch	88	3ª
MARINA II. Urb. Cala'n Bosch	178	3ª
MARIVENT. Urb. Torre del Ram, 10. Tel. 38 07 02	12	3ª
MENORCA-MAR. Urb. Cala'n Bosch	140	3ª
MERCADAL. Urb. Cala Blanca	36	3ª
MONTE VERDE. Urb. Serpentona	24	3ª
NAYBA. Urb. Cala Blanca, p-124-175	16	3ª

Name and Direction	Rooms	Ct.
NURA. Urb. Cala Blanca. Pol. A. P-74-75	32	3ª
ONA. Urb. Serpentona. Parc, 5	24	3ª
OASIS PARK. Urb. Cales Piques, Tel. 38 62 70	509	3ª
PADDLE CLUB VILLAGE. Urb. Cales Piques, 421-424	141	3ª
PINOS, LOS. Urb. Cala Blanca, 147-148. Tel. 28 02 94	48	3ª
PISCIS. Urb. Cala Blanca. Pol. C. Tel. 38 42 76	24	3ª
PLAYA PARC. Urb. Son Xoriguer. Tel. 38 48 81	68	3ª
PROA. Urb. Cap D'Artruix. Par, 2-A. Tel. 38 08 49	42	2ª
RAYMA. Urb. Son Carrió. Parc. 5-F. Tel. 38 13 58 - 38 00 39	16	3ª
RAYMA II. Urb. Son Carrió. Parc, 5-F. Tel. 38 13 58 - 38 00 39	16	3ª
RIO VERDE. Urb. Serpentona. Tel. 37 31 78	48	3ª
ROSA DE LOS VIENTOS. Urb. Son Xoriguer, 62 y 81	96	3ª
ROSALES, LOS. Urb. Los Delfines. Parc. 10 y 11	24	3ª
ROTGER CAMPS I. Urb. Sa Caleta - Santandria. Parc, 12	32	3ª
ROTGER CAMPS II. Urb. Sa Caleta - Santandria. Parc, 14	36	3ª
SA CALA. Urb. Cala Morell	104	3ª
SA CORBA. Urb. Torre del Ram, P-20	32	3ª
SA PUNTA. Urb. Son Carrió. Tel. 38 24 80 - 38 02 52	32	3ª
SA PUNTA II. Urb. Son Carrió. Parc, C	195	3ª
SABINAS I, LAS. Urb. Los Delfines. Tel. 38 12 93	16	3ª
SABINAS II, LAS. Urb. Los Delfines. Tel. 38 12 93	16	3ª
SABINAS III, LAS. Urb. Los Delfines	126	3ª
SES ANCOLLES. Urb. Cala Morell	24	3ª
SES ABEURADES. Urb. Torre del Ram	75	3ª
SES ANNARES. Urb. Cales Piques	72	2ª
SES MALVES. Urb. Cales Piques, P-24	16	3ª
SES ONERETES. Urb. Torre del Ram. Pol. 1	32	3ª
SES PORXADES. Urb. Torre del Ram. Tel. 38 17 45	24	3ª
SES TORRETES. Urb. Cala Blanca	16	3ª
SIMON. Urb. Cala'n Blanes. Tel. 38 04 01	34	3ª
SIESTA-PLAYA. Urb. Tamarinda - Cala'n Bosch. Tel. 38 50 19	343	2ª
SIETE PALMERAS, LAS. Urb. Los Delfines. Pol. II Manz. VI. Parc, 7, 8, 9, 12, y 13. Tel. 38 46 22	140	2ª
SOL DEL SUR. Urb. Son Xoriguer. B-20, B-24	75	2ª
SOL PONENT. Urb. Cala Blanca. Parc. 4. Tel. 38 26 96	38	3ª
SOL Y MAR. Urb. Los Delfines. Tel. 38 21 39	48	2ª
SOLELL. Urb. Serpentona	24	3ª
SOLITALY. Urb. Los Delfines	24	3ª
SON ALMA. Urb. Son Carrió. Tel. 38 46 41	28	3ª
SON BLANCH COTTAGE. Urb. Sa Caleta - Santandria. Tel. 38 00 36 - 38 55 86	259	2ª
SON CARRIO. Urb. Son Carrió. Tel. 38 43 92	36	3ª
SUR LAGO. Urb. Cala'n Bosch. Pol. 1. Parc, 1	140	3ª
SUR MAR. Urb. Cala'n Bosch. Parc, 180	51	3ª
SUR PLAYA. Urb. Cala'n Bosch	252	3ª
SURETS. Urb. Cala Piques, 279. Tel. 38 18 30	28	3ª
TALAIOT, I. Urb. Cales Piques	194	2ª
TALAIOT, II. Urb. Cales Piques	21	3ª
TALAIOT, III. Urb. Cales Piques	57	3ª
TAMARISCOS, LOS. Urb. Calan Bosch	252	2ª
TORRES LLODRA. Urb. Sa Caleta - Santandria	36	3ª
VILLAESCUSA. Urb. Cala Blanca. Pol. x. Parc, 10-11	46	3ª
VISTA BLANCA I. Urb. Cala Blanca. Pol. C. Parc, 8. Tel. 38 20 08	21	3ª
VISTA BLANES. Urb. Calan Blanes	585	2ª
VISTA PLAYA. Urb. Cala Blanca	42	3ª
YUCAS, LAS. Los Delfines. Tel. 38 21 69	98	2ª
ZAFI. Urb. Cala Piques	33	3ª

TELEPHONE NUMBERS

MAÓ

Airport 36 01 50
Red Cross Ambulance 36 11 80
Town Hall 36 98 00
Municipal Information Office 900 30 05 84
Consell Insular 35 15 15
SIAC Menorca 35 44 44
SIAC Palma 900 32 13 21
Delegation of the Government 36 33 51
Guardia Civil 0 62
Health Center 36 04 26
Municipal hospital 36 12 21
Taxi stations 36 28 91
36 12 83
Police station 36 37 12
Police 091
Radio Taxi 36 71 11
Residencia Sanitaria (state hospital) . . 36 35 00

CIUTADELLA

Ambulance Red Cross 38 19 93
Town Hall 38 10 50
Hospital 38 19 14
Guardia Civil 0 62
Local police 38 07 87
Police station 38 10 95
Taxi stations 38 11 97
38 44 35
Radio Taxi 38 28 96
Ambulatory 38 06 87

ALAIOR

Town Hall 37 13 20
Red Cross 37 12 38

ES MERCADAL

Town Hall 37 50 02
Local Police 37 52 51
Guardia Civil 0 62
Red Cross 37 53 00
Radio Taxis 36 71 11

FERRERIES

Town Hall 37 30 03
Local Police 37 40 00
Red Cross 37 31 39
Taxis 37 34 84

SANT LLUIS

Town Hall 15 09 50
Local Police 15 17 17
Taxis 15 40 83

ES CASTELL

Town Hall 36 51 93
Local Police 36 27 47
Taxis 36 27 79

ES MIGJORN GRAN

Town Hall 37 01 10

GENERAL INFORMATION

Historical Data

Beginning of the premegalithic
period . . . . 2.000 a. de C.
Building of the naveta d'es
Tudons . . . . 1.400 a. de C.
Roman conquest . . . . 123 a. de C.
Menorca in the Califat of Córdoba 903
Conquest by Alfonso III 1.287
Menorca goes over the British Crown 1.712
French domination 1.756
New British domination 1.763
Incorporation to the Spanisch Crown 1.802

Demographical Data

Inhabitants in Menorca (in eight Councils) . 61.375
Inhabitants in Maó 22.119
Inhabitants in Ciutadella 19.335

Geographical Data

Surface 701,84 km2
Coastline . . . . 285,04 km.

Distances

Menorca-Alcudia . . . . 104 km.
Menorca-Barcelona . . . . 241 km.
Menorca-Palma de Mallorca . . . . 181 km.
Menorca-Algiers . . . . 388 km.
Menorca-Marseille . . . . 392 km.

Climate in Menorca

Average maximum temperature . . . . . 22-33 ºC
Average minimum temperature . . . . . . 13,90 ºC
Average temperature . . . . 18,11 ºC
Average sunshine hours 2.452
Average humidity 69%

CAR HIRE

MAÓ	Direction	Tel.	SANT LLUIS	Direction	Tel.
ATESA	Aeropuerto de Menorca	369777	AUTOS MENORCA	Punta Prima	360582
AUTOS BISBAL	Plaza España, 13	350772	JOSE COLL PORTELLA.	Conde L'Annion, 39	151731
AUTOS CONFORT	José Anselmo Clavé, 56	369470	JAIME GUAL CERDA	Urbanización S'Algar	151494
AUTOS GABRIEL	José Anselmo Clavé 284	360021	M. GOMILA RIUDAVETS	Punta Prima	365052
AUTOS HNOS. VALLS	Plaza Real, 4	362839	ROY BERNARD FORD	Cap d'en Font	363812
AUTOS ISLA	José Mª Quadrado, 28	366569			
AUTOS MAHON	José Anselmo Clavé, 38		**ES CASTELL**		
AUTOS MENORCA	Plaza Explanada, 73	360582	ANTHONY MARK PERKINS	Santa Bárbara, 44	368074
AUTOS MOMPLE	Explanada, 38	360918	AUTOS ES CASTELL	Carrer Gran, 201	365855
AUTOS MONTE TORO	Virgen de Gracia, 182	360558	AUTOS MENORCA	Urbanización Sol Del Este	360582
AUTOS PONS	José Anselmo Clavé, 157	366879	AUTOS PT	Carrer Gran, 42	364881
AUTOS SAN CLEMENTE	Ctra. San Clemente, km. 5	366857	VALLS FORTUNY	Victori, 43	369119
AUTOS TRAMONTANA	Poima C/ A, 10	361611			
AUTOS VALLS	Plaza Colón, 5	369094			
AUTOS 215	Plaza Retiro, 18 - 2ª	363494	**FERRERIES**		
AUTOS 38	José Anselmo Clavé, 38-A	361394	MIGUEL PONS PONS	Guillermo Coll, 10	373093
AVIS	Aeropuerto de Menorca	361576			
AVIS	Plaza Explanada, 53	364778			
DOCARS	José María Quadrado, 22	360467	**ALAIOR**		
EGGLETON BARRY GRAHAM	Plaza Explanada, 52	362432	AUTOS CALAN PORTER	Doctor Llansó, 73	371331
ELODIA VAZQUEZ SEGUI	Bellavista, 23 - 2ª	365359	GARAJE BALMES	Polígono Industrial	371209
GAVIOTA	Plaza Explanada, 8	360620	GAVIOTA	Polígono Industrial	372555
IBERCARS	Vasallo, 44	364208	IAN WARREN	Urbanización Cala'n Porter	
JANICE MARY MCCLYMONT	Apartado de Correos, 313	367448	PERKINS	Urbanización Cala'n Porter	377290
JUANA MACIAN MERCADAL	Cos de Gracia, 5	365684	VILLA CARS	Miguel de Cervantes, 80	371575
MAGON CARS	Conde de Cifuentes, 34	368515			
M.B. AUTO SPORT	José María Quadrado, 21	350383			
MANUEL VIDAL CANADELL	Camino de la Unión, 12	360123	**CIUTADELLA**		
Mª ESPERANZA FERNANDEZ	Andén de Poniente, 26	360687	AUTOS CONFORT	Avda. Constitución,23	381481
MENOCARS	Vives Llull, 128	363888	AUTOS DIAZ	Paseo del Puerto, 47	382207
MOTOS AVENIDA	José María Quadrado, 39	360529	AUTOS MICAR	Miguel de Cervantes, 77	381574
MOTOS GELABERT	José Anselmo Clavé, 12	360614	AUTOS MIRAMAR	Camí de Maó, 42	383012
MOTOS KIKE	Ciudadela, 71	364120	AVIS	Conquistador, 81	381174
MOTOS MENORCA	Moll de Ponent	367309	BAGUR CASASNOVAS	Conquistador, 72	
MOTOS RAMOS	Andén de Levante, 21	366813	BICICLETAS SALORD	San Isidro, 32	381576
MOTOTURISMO	Plaza Explanada, 54	360880	BLUE CARS	Oriente, 37	380565
OWNERS CARS	Francesc Femenías, s/n	361512	FRIEND CARS	Plaza del Borne, 27	386067
PETER EDWARD BARSBY	Deyá, 2	362698	GARCIA ARGUIMBAU	Camí de Maó, 9	380141
PEDRO PONS GOÑALONS	Poima, B	366629	GAVIOTA	Conquistador, 59	382998
ROBIN NORTON	Camí d'es Castell, 235	364552	MENORCAR	Polígono Industrial	381501
ULTRAMAR CARS	Poima, calle B, 121	369036	MOTOS GENESTAR	C/ Barcelona, 24	382282
VIDAL	José Anselmo Clavé, 2 (motos)	360981	MOTOS MANOLO	Conquistador, 86	385050
			SUNCAR	Alcántara, 39	382290
FORNELLS			VIVO MARQUES	Martorell, 15	383910
ROCA-ROSELLO	Carrer Major, 57	376621			

TRAVEL AGENCIES IN MENORCA

MAÓ	Direction	Tel.	CIUTADELLA	Direction	Tel.
VIAJES BARCELO	Avda. José María Quadrado	360250	VIAJES BARCELON	Camí de Maó, 5	380487
VIAJES COSMELLI	C/ Bastión, 39	363819	VIAJES CIUTADELLA DE MENORCA	C/ Virgen del Carmen, 3	382766
VIAJES CRESTA	Avda. Menorca, 9	368788	VIAJES DORIA	Avda. Conquistador, 21 - B	386262
VIAJES DORIA	Avda. Menorca, 5	368800	VIAJES JAMMA TOURS	C/ Borne, 31	385276
VIAJES EBUSUS	Plaza Explanada, 3	365054	VIAJES RICCI	C/ Purísima, 55	383631
VIAJES EUROPLAN	C/ San Roque, 30	365262	VIAJES ULTRAMAR EXPRESS	Avda. Conquistador, 39	382177
VIAJES ELENA	C/ Santiago Ramón y Cajal, 4	350402	VIAJES OMEGA JET	C/ Conquistador, 101	380040
VIAJES IBERIA	C/ Carrer Nou, 35	362908			
VIAJES IBEROSERVICE	Polígono Industrial, C/D-4-A-2º	363900			
VIAJES MARTEL	Plaza Príncipe, 4	367013			
VIAJES MENORCA TOURS	Plaza Explanada, 59	364150			
VIAJES PONS SANS	Plaza Colón, 6	350885	**ALAIOR**		
VIAJES TIEMPO LIBRE	Dr. Orfila, 58 - 1º	363800	VIAJES JAMMA TOURS	C/ Calvo Sotelo, 26	373802
VIAJES ULTRAMAR EXPRESS	Vassallo, 31	361612	VIAJES CHANGUE TOURS	Urbanización Cala'n Porter	377470
VIAJES WAGONS LITS	Plaza Constitución, 9	364112			

ES CASTELL

VIAJES VILLATOURS	C/ San Jorge, 22 - A	367612

APPROXIMATE DISTANCE IN KMS. BETWEEN POINTS
ON THE ISLAND OF MAJOR INTEREST

km.

From Maó to				km.
From Maó to			Airport	5
>	>	>	Alaior	12
>	>	>	Alcaufar	10
>	>	>	Arenal d'en Castell	19,5
>	>	>	Biniancolla	9,5
>	>	>	Binibeca	9,5
>	>	>	Bisafulla	10
>	>	>	Cala Galdana	40
>	>	>	Cala Mesquida	7
>	>	>	Cala Morell	53
>	>	>	Cala'n Porter	14
>	>	>	Ciutadella	45
>	>	>	Es Castell	3
>	>	>	Es Grao	9
>	>	>	Es Migjorn Gran	22
>	>	>	Ferreríes	29
>	>	>	Fornells	21
>	>	>	Es Mercadal	21
>	>	>	Monte Toro	25
>	>	>	Port D'Addaia	20
>	>	>	Punta Prima	10
>	>	>	S'Algar	10
>	>	>	San Jaime Mediterráneo	18
>	>	>	Sant Lluís	4,5
>	>	>	Santo Tomàs	27,8
>	>	>	Son Bou	16
>	>	>	Son Park	20
From Ciutadella to			Airport	50
>	>	>	Alaior	33
>	>	>	Binibeca	54
>	>	>	Cala Blanca	4
>	>	>	Cala Galdana	27
>	>	>	Cala Morell	8
>	>	>	Cala'n Porter	45
>	>	>	Cala Santandría	3
>	>	>	Cala Turqueta	11,5
>	>	>	Cap d'Artrutx	10
>	>	>	Es Castell	48
>	>	>	Es Migjorn Gran	23
>	>	>	Ferreries	16
>	>	>	Fornells	33
>	>	>	Maó	45
>	>	>	Es Mercadal	24
>	>	>	Monte Toro	29
>	>	>	Port D'Addaia	45
>	>	>	Punta Prima	54
>	>	>	Sant Lluís	49
>	>	>	Santo Tomàs	28
>	>	>	Son Bou	37
From Cala Galdana to			Airport	45
>	>	>	Alaior	27
>	>	>	Arenal d'en Castell	36
>	>	>	Cala'n Porter	40
>	>	>	Cap d'Artrutx	37
>	>	>	Ciutadella	27
>	>	>	Es Castell	43
>	>	>	Ferreries	11
>	>	>	Fornells	28
>	>	>	Maó	40
>	>	>	Es Mercadal	19
>	>	>	Monte Toro	24
>	>	>	Sant Lluís	44,4
>	>	>	Santo Tomàs	22

INDEX